SO-AAC-374

Everyday Ethics
Putting Values into Action

Michael Rion, Ph.D.

Resources for Ethics & Management
West Hartford, Connecticut

Cover Design

The intersecting circles in the cover and logo design represent the interdependence of multiple stakeholders. At the heart of everyday ethics is mutual respect and care. In organizations, we embody this respect by recognizing all those with a "stake" in our actions, such as employees, vendors, customers, communities and stockholders. As we conduct our business inside the center circle, we overlap with the circles of these other stakeholders. These "intersections" mean that we depend on each other to accomplish our goals. When we treat other stakeholders with the respect we, in turn, expect from them, together we build the circles of responsibility that sustain our common life.

Copyright 2002 Michael Rion, Ph.D. All rights reserved.

No part of this book may be reproduced, stored in a retrieval system, or transmitted in any form or by any means– electronic, mechanical, photocopying, recording or otherwise– without the prior written permission of Resources for Ethics and Management.

Printed in the United States of America

Published by
Resources for Ethics and Management
14 Cornell Road
West Hartford, CT 06107-2905
Tel 860-521-9233 Fax 860-521-4697
E-mail mrion@attglobal.net
www.rionethics.com

ISBN 0-9723621-0-X

EVERYDAY ETHICS
An Introductory Note

This book is a practical handbook of ethical behaviors that work -at home, in the community, and especially in the workplace.

The behaviors are ethical because they are rooted in mutual respect. And they work because they are all about cooperation. They enable us together to accomplish shared goals.

I know they work because I have observed these actions in my consulting experience with thousands of employees and managers in a wide variety of industries for more than 20 years.

When people practice these behaviors everyday in organizations, they create an environment of trust, mutual respect and ethical responsibility. This environment, in turn, fosters high levels of productivity and creativity, as well as personal satisfaction.

The practical tips here apply to everyone: individual employees, front line supervisors, middle managers and senior leaders. Although the context is the workplace, virtually all these behaviors are relevant at home and in the community as well.

Some points will simply remind you about things you already know. Others, I expect, will be new insights that will make your day a better one - more productive, more satisfying, even more challenging.

Thanks for making your own commitment to everyday ethics. And if you have ideas to add, let me know!

Michael Rion, Ph.D.

Resources for Ethics and Management

Resources for Ethics and Management helps organizations improve performance and strengthen responsible decision making through practical application of ethical principles and encouragement of values-driven behaviors.

Principal Michael Rion is recognized nationally for his pioneering work in ethics training that bridges the gap between theory and practice. Frequently in demand as a dynamic speaker and trainer, he has led hundreds of workshops for managers and employees at all levels and consulted on ethics and values with major corporations, government and community groups.

Dr. Rion, who earned a Ph.D. in ethics from Yale University, served four years as Director of Corporate Responsibility at Cummins Engine Company and six years as President of Hartford Seminary prior to forming Resources for Ethics and Management in 1989.

Acknowledgements

My colleague Alex Kopper contributed significantly to the ideas presented here, as well as provided expert editorial and graphic design support. Raymond Andrews, Jr. created all the cartoons. Sherry Poulson developed the graphics and layout that enhance the text. My wife Nancy C. Rion applied her editorial expertise to improve the text at every point. I am deeply grateful to them. My sincere thanks also to Robert Gebing, Vice President for Business Practices at Olin Corporation, and to Louise Backer for many helpful ideas as I developed this book.

CONTENTS

Act decisively on problems.

Learn from mistakes.

1. Building Trust

Mutual trust is the "bed rock" for everyday ethics. When we do the right thing, we help create an atmosphere of mutual respect and trust that fosters improved productivity and high levels of ethical responsibility.

Ethics is a participatory activity. Treating a co-worker fairly, answering a customer's complaint honestly, or keeping your promise to someone –actions like these encourage others to respond in kind. When each of us does our part, we express our own integrity and help weave a fabric of shared values and mutual achievement.

Building trust by acting responsibly creates an environment that releases the full potential of each individual to work with others for both personal and organizational success.

Personal commitment and trust makes a safer plant

"I am my brother's keeper" is a key theme in the safety program at one company's chemical plant. Every employee –and every visitor to the site– is encouraged to take responsibility for sensible safety practices that protect everyone.

A cross-functional team representing union and management from all departments fosters the commitment. They identify potential issues and develop solutions before safety problems occur, and they learn from one another when there is disagreement.

The team members encourage all employees, beginning with themselves, to write down a specific personal commitment related to safety in the plant, in the community and at home.

The result: a safer plant environment and a strong sense of pride and mutual accomplishment throughout the plant.

Trust each other to be capable and responsible.

Expect commitment from each other.

Ethics means recognizing our interdependence. That's a big word for a simple idea: we're all in this together, at work and in our personal lives.

Think, for a moment, what your life would be like if you couldn't rely on others. Can the babysitter handle your two-year old as promised? Is your prescription from the pharmacy really what the doctor ordered? Has the elevator been inspected regularly for safety? Will the promised material for your next task arrive? Is your boss serious about this assignment or is it a "set-up?"

A day filled with questions like these is, to say the least, unlikely to be productive.

Count on each other to do your best, and you can achieve challenging goals. You earn trust, participate in shared accomplishments and experience the deep satisfaction of knowing you've done your part.

Sure, there might be an individual who "slacks off." But that's the exception when everyone expects the best from co-workers.

Plus, honest feedback comes more easily in an environment of trust. You can offer constructive feedback and suggestions for improvement, encouraging the under-performing colleague to try harder.

When we expect each other to do the right thing, when we help each other figure it out, and when we support each other in tough situations, we strengthen mutual trust and effectiveness.

Only people are real.

Only people can do research.

Only people have ideas.

Money is a help and machinery is a help, but they are inanimate creations of human beings.

The real achievement is the creative and collective achievement of individuals working together.

—J. Irwin Miller,
Former CEO, Cummins Engine Company

Value diversity.

Building trust also means recognizing everyone's contribution. Diverse skills, personalities, and backgrounds enrich our life and work together.

Consider the evolution of diversity initiatives. First comes fairness– ensuring that no one is excluded because of factors like race and gender. Subtle but powerful habits and assumptions can unintentionally block the full participation of those who seem "different." That's why fairness demands active, affirmative efforts to ensure full inclusion.

Then, organizations try to meet changes in the workforce. The employer that provides the best environment for diverse people will tap the largest pool of potential employees.

And finally comes the best part: diversity helps you solve problems and improve products and processes. Appreciating diversity –not passively "accepting" it but actively fostering it– taps new ideas and different perspectives to generate better solutions.

Seek out the ideas and opinions of all your colleagues. Learn to appreciate the contributions of people who are different from you. Be alert to new perspectives and unexpected opportunities.

Valuing diversity unleashes the full potential of human energy and imagination as we work together.

Listening is not just waiting for your next turn to speak.

—Anonymous

Listen first and well.

Listen and ask questions.

Listening means actively seeking to understand an idea or concern.

If you're too focused on your own ideas or skeptical about the other person, you won't hear what they're saying. As a result, you may jump to conclusions and make false assumptions.

When you genuinely listen, you foster positive relationships and mutual respect. As an Olin Corporation brochure puts it, "It's important to realize that we have two ears and one mouth. Using them in their natural proportion is the recipe for communicating successfully."[1]

Give your full attention to the other person –don't shuffle papers, reach for the phone or shift your body in ways that suggest you're not really interested. Listen actively by asking questions, seeking ideas and encouraging feedback.

Listening enables you to understand others, identify and resolve problems, gain new insights and develop new ideas together.

When we genuinely listen to each other, mutual understanding and creative problem solving flourish.

*For every human problem,
there is a solution that is
simple, neat and wrong.*

—H.L. Mencken

Respect and learn from disagreements.

When we disagree –about an ethical issue, a technical problem, a policy or a business strategy– it's important not only to listen to others but also to learn from them.

When we disagree about ethics, it is tempting to judge the other person. I know I'm right, so you must be wrong. But wait –before jumping to conclusions, consider that both of you are trying to do the right thing. Perhaps you can learn from each other.

This doesn't mean giving up your own convictions. It does mean asking yourself some questions.

Is there something you don't know? You may simply be operating from different facts. A new piece of information might change everything.

Can you learn something from the other person's approach? Some people are highly intuitive, others want to spell things out carefully. Some emphasize consequences, others focus on rules and principles. Learning how the other person is reasoning will help you grasp a different view and, often, shed new light on your own thinking.

Is your perspective limited by your role? Jobs and "social" roles (like economic background, race, and gender) shape how you see things. That's why asking this question might help you see a bigger picture.

For instance, marketing people will nearly always be more flexible about meals, gifts and entertainment than will purchasing people. People from diverse cultural backgrounds may view certain physical greetings (handshakes, hugs, kisses on the cheek) differently, and therefore interpret sexual harassment policies somewhat differently. Diverse roles bring diverse perspectives that enrich your understanding and ideas.

Genuinely respecting other opinions leads to new insight and better solutions.

9

Share information openly and honestly.

Actively offer information –don't hold it back.

Working well together requires a free flow of information and ideas.

Providing information and ideas to co-workers helps them accomplish tasks and encourages them to share as well. Maybe you see an improvement that someone else overlooked. Perhaps your piece of information is critical to a colleague trying to anticipate and meet difficult deadlines. It might turn out that your sharing reminds the other person to fill you in on something else.

It's not like playing poker. There are no points for bluffing. Sometimes people forget this and act as if work relationships are some kind of zero-sum game. In those games –such as poker– a winning strategy includes withholding information and trying to deceive playing partners. If your goal is to win such a game, the strategy works.

But on the job, you rely on others for mutual success. Holding back information is as harmful as actively misleading your co-workers. Either way, you make it harder to accomplish the job.

Contributing your ideas and knowledge actively, on the other hand, can open new possibilities for creative solutions that neither you nor your co-workers could have recognized alone.

When we offer ideas and information, we create an environment of openness that builds trust as well as effectiveness.

Honest feedback is only fair.

Fred's performance has been under par for some time now. He irritates his co-workers instead of cooperating, and he barely meets the minimum objectives on his job description.

A new supervisor decides it's time to terminate Fred, only to discover that past performance reviews have been positive. No one was willing to confront Fred about his behavior and weak performance –it seemed easier to avoid a difficult conversation and hope the problem would go away.

Is it fair to terminate Fred now? Of course not. The company failed to give him honest feedback. Who knows if that feedback would have made a difference, but the past supervisor failed even to try.

Honest, even if tough, feedback shows respect for Fred and gives him a chance –with appropriate help– to improve his performance.

Give honest feedback.

We don't want to hurt people's feelings, but neither should we ignore poor job performance. Respect for the individual means giving honest feedback.

Suppose a co-worker always gets the job done at the last minute, greatly inconveniencing others. But your colleague, a nice person, apologizes every time. It's tempting to accept the apologies to avoid conflict.

But ignoring the problem –or worse, just complaining about it to others –may simply postpone an inevitable confrontation that will only be worse the longer you wait. And you miss the chance to help your co-worker improve performance. Better to explain, kindly but plainly, the difficulty the lateness causes others. Then you can work together on solutions.

If you are a supervisor, use performance assessment procedures to provide honest feedback. No one is well served by vague generalizations in performance discussions. Far more helpful is specific, candid feedback on what areas need improvement.

Giving timely, candid and sensitive performance feedback treats people with respect and fosters positive improvement.

"Blowing the Whistle"

One Fortune 500 company lost substantial government business in a scandal that could easily have been prevented if even one person had raised a question early in the process. There are countless similar examples in front-page stories of business ethics scandals.

Sometimes speaking up means reporting a serious problem, doing so even at great personal risk.

Responsible companies make every effort to enable employees to report such problems without fear of retaliation. They provide multiple channels of communication, including anonymous telephone lines, and they adopt policies to protect employees who speak up. As one CEO put it, "If I find someone 'shooting the messenger,' I'll shoot that person myself."

But speaking up doesn't just apply to dramatic instances that we may read in the headlines.

It also means making suggestions for improvement, challenging actions or policies where there is legitimate and open disagreement about the best approach, and encouraging an atmosphere of honest dialogue.

Speak up.

Challenge the process.

If something doesn't make sense, we need to tell somebody–a supervisor, another manager, someone else in the organization, even the telephone help line if there is one.

Many examples of corporate "scandals" could easily have been avoided if even one person had spoken up early on. But it is human nature to resist getting involved.

This was famously demonstrated in tragic fashion in New York City many years ago. A young woman named Kitty Genovese was murdered in an apartment courtyard while 30 to 40 people who heard the commotion or saw the attack did nothing -no one screamed, no one called the police.

That tragedy reminds us how vitally important it is to speak up when we see something wrong. In the workplace, the stakes are equally high if the problem involves product safety or environmental hazards. The explosion of the space shuttle Challenger due to a faulty gasket brought this home dramatically.

Other problems are not fatal but they still affect the lives and livelihoods of employees, customers and stockholders. The "blockbuster" failure of Enron beginning late in 2001 is a recent and vivid illustration.

Speaking up doesn't guarantee the organization will do the right thing. According to press accounts, internal "whistleblowers" at Enron did alert management to the problems to no avail. But at least you should try to do your part.

Speaking up not only helps the organization. It also means we can sleep better at night knowing we didn't duck our responsibility.

Be outraged.

Silence in the face of ethical doubts implies our consent to possibly unethical actions. Rationalizations like "everyone is doing it" or "profits are more important than ethics" can dull our sensitivity to right and wrong.

If something is clearly wrong, say so. One senior executive tells colleagues to look for people with a "capacity for moral outrage." That means people who will speak up when they see something questionable rather than stay quiet for fear of being seen as troublemakers.

Of course, it's always wise to think twice and not jump to conclusions. "Crying wolf" in righteous indignation will quickly undermine your credibility with colleagues when your facts are wrong or there is another side to the story.

But it is important to balance this sound advice with a keen sense of when to express legitimate outrage at unethical behavior. Organizational leaders need to foster an open environment that encourages and supports responsible people who are willing to speak up.

When we listen to our heart and find the courage to speak up when it really matters, both the organization and we are better for it in the long run.

Think what others ought to be like, then start being like that yourself.

—Anonymous

Treat others fairly.

Give and receive mutual respect.

The "Golden Rule" has it right: we should treat others as we would like to be treated.

When you do that, it works for everyone. As a consumer, don't you trust retailers who have treated you fairly when there have been product flaws or complaints? As an employee, wouldn't you rather work for an organization that demonstrates fair treatment to all employees? No matter what the outcome on a specific matter, you rightly expect to be treated with courtesy and respect.

The same holds true in personal relationships. When trying to decide what's fair –whether dividing the workload on house cleaning day, choosing vacation destinations amid conflicting desires and schedules, or dividing family heirlooms on the death of elderly parents– you want to be heard and respected in the process. If you take seriously each other's interests and viewpoints, you build confidence in the fairness of the outcome.

When we treat each other with courtesy and respect, we build a sense of fairness and trust.

Ethics at work is often not the simple choice of right versus wrong, but of reconciling competing "rights."

Be objective.

Fair decisions use criteria that are clearly appropriate to the specific issue.

If you're deciding who has to work on New Year's Eve, criteria might include taking turns on various holidays or whose skills are most needed for the particular job. But the fact that one person is a relative shouldn't be a consideration!

Fairness means treating people equally unless there are relevant differences between them. Objectivity means identifying which differences matter, and which do not, in a specific situation.

For the right to vote in the United States, we agree that only a few differences are relevant such as age and legal status. But when we determine salaries, other differences may be relevant such as performance, skill or experience.

Decisions based on mutually agreed categories help ensure a sense of fairness. Even if you disagree with the ultimate judgment, it is easier to accept when you are confident that the decision-maker consistently used only acceptable considerations and did not "play favorites."

Objective treatment earns the trust and confidence that enables all of us to work together constructively.

Seek creative options for special circumstances.

Sometimes rigid consistency yields a technically fair decision that violates common sense. Fairness includes openness to special situations.

A dramatic example of this flexibility is the decision by some firms who lost employees in the World Trade Center tragedy to extend compensation and benefits to families beyond what might technically be required.

On a less dramatic scale, the same consideration of unique circumstances sometimes comes into play when an employee is terminally ill or a severed employee faces unusual health costs. There are no clear rules for "exceptions," but we all know there are times when special treatment is simply the right thing to do.

Fairness builds trust and confidence when there is room for creativity and sensitivity to unusual situations.

Always do right.
This will gratify some and
astonish the rest.

– Mark Twain

Keep your word.

Say what you'll do, and do what you say.

We depend on each other in a fast-paced business environment.

If you can't count on the commitments of co-workers, your own tasks will suffer. Likewise, if you fail to make and keep commitments, others will lose confidence in you.

Each of us depends on promise keeping in all sorts of ways every day. You expect the newspaper at the door in the morning; your child knows you will pick him or her up after school just as you promised; your dentist assumes you'll keep your appointment; your customers know you will make your presentation in the conference room at the scheduled time. In most of these day-to-day experiences, you don't even think of "making a promise." You just do what you said you would do.

Sometimes, the commitment is more dramatic. You promise rush delivery of a vital product to a customer; you make good on your commitment to attend your child's school performance; you show up when you said you would to assist a work team on an urgent project.

Each of these actions –mundane or dramatic–helps to build bonds of trust. Every time you say what you'll do and do what you say, you deepen those bonds.

When we keep our promises, we earn the trust of others.

26

Don't make promises you can't keep.

Sometimes we get pressure to over-promise.

Don't say you'll do something if you can't do it.

It is only natural to tell your child you'll "be there" when the child pleads with you. But if it is unlikely that you can show up, be honest rather than holding out unrealistic hope. Anytime you say what you'll do and then fail, you undermine trust and create doubts about your reliability.

It's tempting at work, for example, to propose an unrealistic performance target or to promise a delivery date that is too big a stretch. Or, your boss over-promises and leaves you to fulfill it. This creates ethical dilemmas later if you can't keep the promise. You may even be tempted to make compromises such as filing false reports or shipping flawed products. Better to be honest from the outset.

Inspiring targets are perfectly appropriate in any organization that strives to excel. Responsible people accept the challenge, but they also recognize the line between "stretch" goals that encourage high performance and unrealistic expectations that are likely to lead to disappointment.

When we avoid making promises we can't keep, we build trust and avert potential problems later.

Some people never make a mistake, nor do they ever make anything else.

–Anonymous

Accept responsibility when you fall short.

People judge our integrity as much by how we handle a mistake as by our ability to avoid mistakes.

Sometimes you fall short –we all do. It might be as simple as missing a meeting due to a flat tire or as significant as failing to deliver to a major customer despite a good faith effort.

Speak up as soon as possible to explain and apologize. Then do whatever is appropriate to make up for the problem. Sometimes a simple apology is enough – a phone call to explain a missed appointment, a sincere explanation to your child about a missed activity. In other circumstances, more may be required.

Penalty clauses in contracts and warranty commitments for consumer products are some of the practices businesses have developed to respond when their performance falls short. Individually, you might need to devote extra time or rearrange your schedule to make up for missing a deadline.

When you "step up" and deal honestly with the issue right away, you are doing the right thing and earning the respect and trust of the other person for your candor and integrity.

We all make mistakes. Accepting responsibility and taking corrective action builds credibility for depending on each other again.

2. Living Our Values

Together we sustain trust by first understanding and then living the practical day to day meaning of our shared values and commitments. That means doing the right thing every time.

It starts with a clear commitment to responsible shared values and the personal integrity to sustain that commitment in the midst of daily pressures. It means using our head and our heart to recognize and resolve tough questions.

When we teach children to be responsible, we start with specific behaviors like being polite, respecting other people's belongings and so on. Over time children "practice" these actions until they become automatic. Being responsible means taking responsible actions; taking those actions regularly helps shape patterns of responsible behavior.

It's the same with ethics at work. As individuals, we practice responsible behaviors in all our interactions. If everyone does this -and the organization reinforces it–everyday ethics becomes institutionalized.

When we take responsibility to know and do the right thing, our actions give life to our values and foster the mutual trust at the heart of everyday ethics.

Be careful what you say.

It's tempting to declare high sounding values, to set admirable policies, and to sign on to challenging goals. But if you're not serious, don't even start. What happens, for example, when...

- A new ethics policy is distributed, but employees see unchallenged violations in their department?

- Senior management proclaims a commitment to respecting personal and family life, but the pressures for arriving early, staying late and working on weekends continue unabated?

- Quality is touted as the number one priority, but compromises are made daily to meet production quotas?

- Integrity is cited as a core value, yet people with questionable ethics but good numbers are promoted?

Say what you really mean and then do it. You'll earn trust and foster commitment. Otherwise, just don't say it.

Let your actions speak louder than words.

Develop and honor shared values.

Shared values like integrity, excellence, customer service and respect help us achieve success together.

When the core values are clear, you can pursue ambitious goals. Because you know what really matters, you're not threatened by changes in strategy and technology. That's why shared values help drive extraordinary long-term performance according to a major study of successful companies.[2]

Not every set of shared values is necessary ethical. This leads some organizations into trouble –key players share common values but they focus too narrowly on self-interest and end up with ethical failure, public scandals and legal penalties.

Shared values may be articulated in formal documents or simply developed informally through the culture of the organization. The focus is not on "word smithing" but on day to day actions that bring the values to life. You bring "Integrity" to life when you insist on handling a tough situation in the right way. Your supervisor gives practical meaning to a "Respect" commitment when he or she takes seriously your ideas and suggestions.

Resolving an ethics problem can also demonstrate shared values. For instance, a manufacturing company charged with price-fixing immediately contacted affected customers and offered generous financial settlements. The original problem resulted from one or two "bad apples" in a regional office and the company could have delayed settlements through court battles. Instead, they focused first on fixing the problem and demonstrated that integrity really mattered in the conduct of their business.

When we know who we are and what we stand for together, we can face challenges with commitment and creativity.

33

Conscience, that stuff can drive you nuts.

–Terry, in <u>On the Waterfront</u>

Act responsibly.

Set real standards of behavior, not just words on posters and in codes of conduct, by acting responsibly and expecting the same from others.

"Walk the talk" is a tired cliché, but the advice is no less wise for being familiar. The trick is actually to do it every day, all the time. One responsible action is worth a thousand words in policies and speeches.

When you credit the contribution of a co-worker, teamwork and trust values come alive.

When your supervisor immediately stops production to address a potential hazard, the safety value leaps from the poster into day to day plant life.

And when an executive ensures that profit sharing applies equitably to all employees –not just to senior managers– values like respect and fairness are credibly at work.

Just as these positive behaviors reinforce shared values, inconsistent actions undermine confidence and commitment. If you cut corners, treat others disrespectfully, or fail to accept responsibility for a problem, shared values are weakened whether you are the CEO or a fellow front line employee.

The same thing is true in your life outside work. If you tell your child to be honest and then the child sees you giving a dishonest answer to another adult, your credibility plummets. If your local elected representative campaigns on an issue and follows through when elected, you have more faith than in the official who says one thing and does another.

When our actions demonstrate the values we profess, we earn credibility with one another and strengthen our shared commitment.

Responsible decision making yields a return on values directly proportional to organizational commitment.

Tell the stories that keep shared values alive.

Be alert to "success stories" that show how people do the right thing.

It might be the lucrative business deal turned down for ethical concerns, or the worker who spotted a potential safety hazard and went the "extra mile" to get it fixed. Or, it could be the less dramatic but equally powerful stories of employees simply doing their jobs well every day despite unusual pressures. When you "catch" a co-worker doing the right thing, congratulate the person and share the example with others.

There are also success stories about ethical problems. When you learn that the company acted decisively to correct a problem –refunding to customers without hassles, bringing a pollution control mechanism up to standard quickly, terminating a supervisor who pressured employees to cut a corner– your confidence in shared values increases.

Formal communication about values through videos and posters helps, but the most powerful messages occur through telling these stories.

Telling these (true!) stories encourages everyone and renews our shared commitment.

Your first ethical obligation is to be good at what you do.

Contribute fully.

Know your job and do it well.

It's up to each of us to make our organization successful <u>and</u> ethical. Personal responsibility starts by giving "an honest day's work for an honest day's pay."

This is especially true in today's global economy. A small rural-based company in India or Italy can compete with the very best from businesses around the world. That's why each of us needs to bring our best knowledge, skills and commitment to our job. It's also why organizations try to develop employees through ongoing training to ensure that skills and knowledge keep up with rapid change.

Failure to do your job well invites ethical problems.

For instance, a misunderstood work order results in a safety flaw in the product; an accounting error combined with relentless pressure for quarterly results lead to "fiddling" the numbers; or the simple failure to produce a good product at a reasonable costs requires tough choices about layoffs and plant closings.

On the other hand, doing your job well builds trust and mutual gain.

The employee who solves a customer's problem builds a strong bond that helps keep a long-term relationship. The accountant who fully understands the relevance of technical procedures prevents the company from making a serious and costly error. And the manufacturing employee who speaks up about a marginal quality problem now heads off serious safety problems later.

When each of us does our share, together we build personal and organizational success.

Whether you think you can or think you can't, you're right.

–Henry Ford

Go beyond what's expected.

Doing our jobs well also means taking the initiative to do things better, to go beyond normal expectations.

Sometimes, in the midst of the rapid pace of work or the detailed procedures that define your job, it's easy to take a narrow focus. If you just check off this procedure or get through this next problem, you've done enough today.

But you'll achieve much more, and you'll take more pride in your own contributions, if you go further whenever you can.

If you see something wrong, speak up. If you have a new idea, share it. If you can work harder and smarter to achieve a goal, do it. Challenge common assumptions, "go the extra mile," and surprise your customer or your co-worker with your positive efforts.

You'll probably surprise yourself, too, with personal growth and achievements you didn't think possible. Stretching yourself to learn a new task or achieve a difficult target brings personal satisfaction. Accomplishing something you once thought impossible can be an enormous source of personal pride and self-motivation.

Ordinary people achieve extraordinary results when we use our full potential instead of holding back.

If you burn down your neighbor's house, it doesn't make yours look better.

–Lou Holtz

Focus on solutions, not on turf.

Fight for ideas and solutions, not credit. "Turf battles" are unproductive and disheartening.

Your ego gets involved when you have an idea. It's not just a suggestion, it is *your* idea. The other department's approach is not just different, it is *their* proposal. *They* are trying to expand their control and status; *we* are defending our power and position.

You may have to fight these "turf battles" in a hostile, highly political work environment. But never forget that you're fighting the wrong "war." An organization that rewards turf victories fails to tap the very best its people can offer.

Far better –for the quality of the outcome and for the satisfaction of all employees– is to seek solutions without regard to position and politics.

Offer your ideas and be open to the ideas of others. Work together to find solutions that best serve the need. See your success through others as well as through your own actions.

We succeed together when we offer ideas openly and look for effective solutions, not personal credit and political points.

When you come to a fork in the road, take it.

– Yogi Berra

See the principles behind the rules.

Know the rules, of course.

Comply with the code of conduct and other policies.

You should know the rules that apply to your job and where to turn for help if you're puzzled. These rules help ensure consistent decisions across the company and reinforce the commitment to responsible behavior.

Imagine what would happen if each member of an orchestra played from different pieces of music. Or, how would a baseball game proceed if one team expected four outs in each inning, while the competitor assumed only three? Chaos would be the result.

That's why you need to know the "rules of the game" in your workplace. Some actions are clearly off-limits –as with certain conflict of interest policies, for instance—and some procedures are mandatory to ensure compliance with both company and regulatory requirements. It's your responsibility to understand how these rules apply to you.

When we know and follow the applicable rules, we maintain the consistency necessary for compliance and ethical responsibility.

Ask the Right Questions.

1. Why is this bothering me?

   Is it really an issue? Am I genuinely perplexed or am I afraid to do what I know is right?

2. Who else matters?

   Who are the stakeholders who may be affected by my decisions? The Golden Rule still works!

3. Is it my responsibility?

   What is my role? What are my obligations? Should I do more in this case?

4. What is the ethical concern?

   Legal obligation, company policy, fairness, promise keeping, honesty, doing good, avoiding harm? The list is not long or complicated.

5. What do others think?

   Who can I ask for advice? Can I learn from those who disagree with my judgment?

6. Am I being true to myself?

   What kind of person or company would do what I am contemplating? Could I share my decision in good conscience with my family? With colleagues and public officials?

For more about these Guidelines for Ethical Decision Making, see Michael Rion, <u>The Responsible Manager</u> (Resources for Ethics and Management, 1999).

No rulebook is thick enough.

It's impossible to write detailed rules for every situation. We still have to make judgment calls.

Reliance on rules alone, in fact, undermines personal responsibility and sound judgment. If you assume there is a rule for everything, two things can occur, both of them dangerous.

Your sense of moral responsibility might grow numb; the rules tell you what to do in such detail that you absolve yourself of personal responsibility. You no longer recognize underlying ethical principles, so you might miss serious problems that don't fit the rules. A required lab procedure, for instance, might have an unanticipated consequence with safety implications. But the standard operating procedure does not address it, so you are slow to recognize and respond to the problem.

Or, you might assume that "anything goes" if the rules are silent. You become so accustomed to rules-based behavior that you forget to apply ethics to actions and decisions when there are no rules. For example, there are so many safety related procedures that, when there is no procedure, you take careless actions on the assumption that "they would have given us a procedure if we needed it."

Taking responsibility means recognizing when black and white blurs to gray.

Reasonable people with integrity may reach different conclusions in these gray areas. But if you ask the right questions in the tough cases, you are more likely to make thoughtful, ethically responsible decisions.

Knowing the rules is critical, but making responsible decisions when the rules are silent or ambiguous strengthens compliance and ethics in the organization.

Emphasize the "why" behind the rules.

There are (or should be!) good reasons for the rules.
Knowing those reasons can deepen our commitment.

If you only emphasize the rules without explaining the "why," you send the wrong message to co-workers who want to do the right thing. You also risk compliance problems. A "check the box" mentality focuses more attention on monitoring for mistakes and violations than on reinforcing positive commitment. The result can be reluctant obedience rather than real dedication.

When you respect others as responsible adults by explaining the purpose behind the rules, you encourage personal responsibility.

The reason might be specific regulatory requirements, so that a seemingly trivial rule (such as entering an "x" rather than a check mark on a documentation form) can be explained by the consequences of failing a government audit.

More often, the particular rules are grounded in a principle that you can affirm even if you would not have written the same rule. Policies on meals, gifts and entertainment, for example, are based on ethical concerns about avoiding undue influence or the appearance of such influence. That principle applies even if the rules are vague or differ between departments.

If you don't agree with a rule in the company's code, it is easier to comply in good faith when you understand why the rule was adopted. Compliance is not just "because we said so;" it is because you want to have a consistent way of acting on a deeper principle. Then you can support the "spirit" as well as the "letter" of the rules.

When we know the reasons for the rules, we achieve strong compliance and we make responsible decisions when the rules aren't clear.

49

"Hot Line" or "Help Line"?

Most large companies now offer toll free telephone lines for employees to raise concerns outside the normal "chain of command." There are two basic approaches:

"Hot Lines" focus on reporting problems and are especially important in industries where the regulatory and legal risks of unreported violations are great. The danger here is unintentionally sending the message that it is a "snitch" line only.

"Help Lines" offer a vehicle for answering questions along with inviting employees to report problems. In many cases, there is a way to call back for feedback without giving your name (the same way you use a "PIN" for your bank account). Many large companies contract with an outside organization to handle the calls, thus enabling an added layer of independence and confidentiality.

In all cases, the phone line is a "back up" system. Ideally, communication is good enough that employees and supervisors can solve problems at the local level.

But no organization has perfect communication, so the 1-800 number provides another avenue to help ensure that employees can identify issues before they become major problems.

Ask for help.

Most issues get resolved on the spot when we talk directly with the people involved.

When you have a problem or see something wrong, talk to your peers and supervisor. If you're the supervisor or manager, respect your employees by keeping open channels of communication and responding to concerns fairly. Never underestimate how difficult it is for an employee to raise a tough issue, especially in a high-pressure work environment.

In some cases, you may need to talk to other people, including higher level managers or staff resource people in human resources, compliance or legal. If you've tried with no success to raise an issue with your supervisor or others –or if you are afraid to raise a sensitive issue for fear of retaliation–then by all means call the 800 number if your organization has one. It's there as a "back-stop" to give you another communication channel that can protect your anonymity if necessary.

Asking for help and reporting problems helps all of us resolve concerns before they become significant problems.

Conscience: the still small voice that tells you someone, somewhere, is watching.

– Anonymous

Listen to your heart as well as your head.

If it "feels wrong," stop and think.

It may be your conscience speaking. Honor your heart by thinking it through again.

Be alert for signs of unease. Some people refer to the "sniff" test (does it "smell"?) or the newspaper headline test (would you be comfortable if your decision appeared in the paper?). It's tempting to ignore these twinges of conscience. There may be so much riding on a particular decision that it is scary to challenge it.

But you ignore these insights at your peril. Ignoring something you sense is wrong can create bigger problems later on. In the worst case, picture yourself responding to a hostile court room attorney asking if you had any doubts and why you didn't act on them.

Of course, making decisions based only on your heart could lead to chaos in the workplace –for instance, you can't just decide to reject a particular policy that you don't like.

That's why listening to your heart leads to using your head. Rushing to judgment fosters self-righteous posturing that misses the real issue. Once you're "tuned in" to a concern, examine the issue carefully to make a responsible decision.

When we listen to our heart, we can use our head to make thoughtful decisions.

Be courageous.

When the stakes are high, doing the right thing can be risky. That's when our integrity is really challenged.

You may not expect to be a hero or heroine. But you may be challenged, at some point in your career, to make a tough choice that requires courage. You don't necessarily know your moral strength until you're tested. But you can build your capacity for courage in small ways every day.

Speaking up when it is easier to keep quiet, providing tough honest feedback instead of the easy "white lie," reaching out to help someone else when others are reluctant to do so, going beyond what is expected to raise an important concern –these are just examples of the many ways you build the sinews of courage in your day to day actions.

Courage doesn't mean acting foolishly in the face of overwhelming odds. Don't take risks without thinking it through. But do know where you draw the line and be willing to take a stand when fundamental values are involved. It takes courage, but you'll sleep a lot better at night.

When we take courageous actions, we strengthen our own integrity and contribute to the well being of others.

***When you throw out integrity,
the rest is easy.***

–J.R Ewing ("Dallas" television show)

Encourage the heart.

We didn't get our personal character and integrity –our "heart"—as an injection along with the other childhood vaccines. Others nurtured us, supported us and challenged us —parents, friends and family, as well as community and religious groups and schools.

These relationships are "communities of conscience," small groups of people who sustain your heart. As an adult, you continue to need these relationships. You need people who nurture and support you when you're struggling. And you need people who know you well enough to recognize signs of change, to remind you of your values and hold you accountable if you start to slip. Otherwise, you will eventually "lose heart" by trying to go it alone.

Consider how you develop these communities of conscience in your own life. It may be family, close friends, and religious and community groups. And you may encourage similar relationships among colleagues at work. When you do this at work, together you strengthen not only your own hearts, but the character of the organization as well.

Making time for the things that nurture our heart prevents burn out and sustains the strength of our character.

Balance work with "life."

The personal character enabling us to do the right thing is nurtured and supported by a balanced life.

Pressures at work can undermine this balance. Increased work loads, frequent overtime and constant tight deadlines may burden you. Email, voice mail and portable computing blur the lines between work and personal life.

Don't take personal commitments and relationships for granted. Make time for friends and family, for community involvement, and for leisure activities that nurture you.

And the organization can help. Be sensitive to individual circumstances. Try to encourage the balance –by taking advantage of policies like flexible hours, family leave, on-site day care for employees' children, and time off for community involvement.

A senior executive once commented to me, "If you are what you do, when you don't, you aren't." You are not merely the sum total of what you do on the job –you are a unique individual with opportunities for rich relationships within your workplace and beyond.

When we find the right balance in our own lives, we become fuller persons who make better contributions in everything we do.

Progress might have been all right once, but it has gone on too long.

–Ogden Nash

Maintain a sense of humor.

Listen and learn.

Every work place has its own sense of humor. Enjoy the diversion (so long as it is not mean-spirited or offensive). Humor builds common ties among co-workers and helps us get through tough days.

Pay attention to the unspoken messages too. Do some "running jokes" point to problems that need to be addressed? Are some topics "off-limits" for humor?

Sometimes a little comedy helps people cope with an unsolvable problem, like an unpleasant boss whose position is secure. Scott Adams, creator of the Dilbert cartoon series, developed a comic franchise by tapping this powerful theme in many offices.

Take special note of topics that aren't laughed about. They may be too important to the organization's purpose to treat lightly. But sometimes the fact that something is off-limits is a clue that it needs attention. Acknowledging gaps and challenging the process may be appropriate when a real problem is so serious we don't poke fun at it.

Laughing and listening enable us to appreciate and find ways to improve a positive work environment.

Laugh at yourself.

Ethics is serious business, but stepping back and laughing at ourselves helps keep perspective.

The workday can be tough no matter how good the organization. High-pressure deadlines, heavy workloads and confusing or complicated situations can wear you down. You may start taking yourself too seriously.

When that happens, you can miss the bigger picture. You get preoccupied with an immediate task or problem and overlook other responsibilities. Or you simply get down on yourself —stressed out, overreacting to problems, discouraged and unproductive.

A sense of humor, even about yourself, helps prevent that attitude. Notice when you start taking the world on your shoulders. Join in the humor of your colleagues. Even poke fun at yourself.

Whatever your sense of humor, maintain it to keep a proper, healthy perspective on the pressures of work.

A hearty laugh or a quiet smile sometimes enables us to take a fresh look at things.

Unless someone like you cares a whole awful lot, nothing is going to get better. It's not!

–Dr. Seuss

Take responsibility – ethics is everyone's job.

It's up to each one of us.

Ethics is NOT the job of a staff person in the head office. Ethics happens –or it fails to happen—on the job everyday in every work area.

All the practical suggestions so far come down to living responsibly in every thing you do. You always have the choice to act in ways that satisfy your conscience and fulfill your responsibilities.

And, while you don't control how others act, your consistent, ethically responsible behavior is likely to encourage the same in others.

A Japanese concept, kyosei, captures an essential truth here. The Japanese symbol includes two characters: one reminds us of hands together, the other evokes a living plant. Roughly translated in a literal way, it means "together we live." A business-related definition is "working together for common good."[3]

On either translation, the concept of kyosei reminds us that we depend on each other to thrive and to fulfill our common goals.

Ethics is up to each one of us: not because we do it alone, but because when we each do our part, we succeed together.

66

Support ethics initiatives.

There is a role for formal ethics programs, including the staff people who implement them.

Common steps in large organizations include compliance or ethics officers, training and communication programs, toll-free "hot" or "help" lines and codes of conduct. These actions reinforce shared commitment in the organization and help even the most responsible people sharpen their ability to resolve dilemmas.

Participate actively in training and awareness programs. Offer your ideas in feedback sessions. Take seriously communications about specific policies. Don't be the cynic who looks for the hidden agenda and resists commitment. Accept your own responsibility and remain open to new ideas and new ways to resolve problems.

When each of us does our part, we make the organization and ourselves better.

3. Solving Problems

If we're serious in our commitment and honest with ourselves, we know we sometimes fall short. Maintaining trust includes solving problems and finding ways to improve on a continuous basis.

Leaders –whether senior managers or first line supervisors— need to be in touch with people on the front lines to answer questions like these:

- *Do our actions every day support our stated values?*
- *Do people really believe they can raise questions and report problems without fear of retaliation?*
- *Are we missing opportunities to improve performance?*
- *Are the standards and procedures clear, understandable and helpful?*

And when the answers point to problems, taking decisive action and learning from mistakes will strengthen the organization and build confidence among all employees that we're serious about ethical responsibility.

The actions outlined in this section focus especially on people with leadership and supervisory responsibilities. But each of us can contribute to mutual success by giving honest feedback and acting responsibly in everything we do.

"Open" communications?

Merely attending "question and answer" sessions with a leader doesn't ensure good communication. The leader and the culture need to be genuinely open. If not, you may experience something like this:

Nikita Khrushchev, at a press conference while he was the leader of the Soviet Union, was responding to an anonymous written question.

"The question: What was he, an important figure, doing during all those crimes of Stalin that he had retroactively exposed and denounced? Khrushchev was livid with rage. 'Who asked that question?' he demanded. 'Let him stand up!' Nobody did. 'That's what I was doing,' said Khrushchev."[4]

Ask the People Who Know

Keep informal channels of communication open.

That way, when a tough issue arises, it's not the first time we have talked to each other.

Communication is always a two way street –in fact, it's more like a busy traffic pattern with all sorts of chances to be in touch with one another. Use opportunities like these:

- Senior leaders: regularly walk through the work site or eat in the cafeteria to greet employees at all levels and encourage informal comments and feedback;
- Supervisors: stay in touch with employees by asking sensitive questions, dropping into break rooms, grabbing lunch with an employee you haven't talked with in a while;
- Employees: take advantage of these informal contacts to develop confidence and comfort with supervisors and leaders;
- Everyone: use email to reach others in the organization to ask questions or make suggestions.

Informal interaction helps leaders stay in touch with the "pulse" of things, fosters open communication with employees and makes it easier to raise a difficult issue without feeling intimidated.

Potential problems often disappear if we're using regular and candid two-way communication.

To be good is noble. To teach others to be good is nobler ...and no trouble.

–Mark Twain

Develop periodic forums for open "give and take."

In the midst of busy work schedules, it's easy to get focused on immediate tasks and overlook developing problems. Taking a step back to talk about the work minimizes the risk of unanticipated problems.

If you're a supervisor or manager, schedule occasional sessions for people to ask questions, make suggestions, and raise issues. If you're invited to such a meeting, take it seriously: offer your ideas, raise your concerns and questions.

Scheduled discussions add a critical dimension to informal channels. They ensure that you get a chance to provide feedback and that you are reminded how important it is to speak up. The more regularly and honestly you deal with each other in this way, the more you tap the full potential of every person and enable discovery of the best solutions.

You know how true this is in personal relationships as well. Couples, families and friends often find it helps to schedule time to discuss important issues in the relationship. Otherwise, the hectic pace of activities and commitments can turn small misunderstandings or disagreements into major points of tension.

When we participate in open forums with candor and responsible follow up, we gain new insights while deepening our shared commitment.

Workplace pressure should never put ethics "on hold."

Ask everybody with surveys.

In large organizations, we can also ask the people who know using surveys.

Be prepared to act on the results; otherwise, don't even ask.

If you're an employee who is surveyed, give honest feedback, expect to hear about the results, and keep asking supervisors and managers what actions have been taken.

Surveys enable you to hold each other accountable for fulfilling your values. The trends and the commitments to particular actions provide benchmarks that anyone –from the CEO to the front line employee– can refer to in asking questions and seeking updates.

If you're a manager, surveys can help you pay attention to how you're doing in living your shared values. Tracking trends and being alert to emerging issues helps you resolve matters before they become major problems. When the results are encouraging, use the occasion for celebrating and reinforcing a positive environment.

Asking questions and acting responsibly on the answers solves problems and builds trust.

Man does not live by words alone, despite the fact that sometimes he has to eat them.

–Adlai Stevenson

Respect and learn from the skeptics.

How often does a "Dilbert" cartoon ring true in the workplace? Scott Adams, the creator of this popular series, taps into the "dark side" of many offices with a healthy dose of good humor.

Take the skeptics seriously because there is always room for improvement.

Skeptics are not cynics. The difference is simple. Cynics are usually bitter and scornful, mocking the beliefs and actions of others. The cynic's mind is made up and it's usually negative.

Skeptics, on the other hand, are simply doubtful and questioning when they see actions that seem inconsistent with stated values. The skeptic still shares the values and, like the canary in the mineshaft that is affected first by poisonous gas, the skeptic provides early warning that can protect the organization's health.

If you're the skeptic, recognize the value of your questions without falling into cynicism. If you work with skeptics, affirm and learn from them so that they have no reason to become cynics.

When we respect each other and listen to tough questions from skeptics, we avoid problems and strengthen our shared values.

Reward Responsible Behaviors Even When the Numbers Are Off

Develop and promote responsible people.

Supporting people who act responsibly strengthens ethics and trust in the organization. If people who achieve good business results by cutting corners are rewarded instead, it's hard to maintain ethical commitment.

You must be vigilant. In the midst of rapid change and fierce pressures for quarterly results, your attention gets focused on matters like productivity, efficiency, cost-effectiveness, revenue generation and so on. That's why it's so important to remember the ethics and values dimensions as well.

Compliment an individual for raising an ethical issue in a meeting. Praise an employee who does a task in ways that show your values. Give these values "equal time" with more technical business considerations in performance reviews and development plans.

When we reward and affirm responsible actions, our commitment to ethics comes alive.

Ethical dilemmas often arise as the unintended consequences of well-intentioned actions, not from unethical motives.

Align incentives with ethics.

Pay attention to reward systems that might tempt people to make poor ethical decisions.

It is often the unintended consequences of well-intentioned plans that create ethical dilemmas. For instance, an aggressive performance plan with impossible goals may lead some people to "fudge numbers" to help the whole department meet a goal. Or, on a personal level, your need to pay the mortgage and your education loans might lead you to cut a corner to preserve your job. The intention is positive –to encourage and challenge people with "stretch" goals, to meet your financial obligations– but the unintended ethical lapse may result.

If you're a leader, be alert to these predictable tendencies and design incentive programs that minimize the risks. How results are achieved –ethically, in compliance with regulations, consistent with shared values– is as important as achieving the numbers. Tie incentives to tough but realistic goals and include the "how" as well as the result.

As an employee, never use the pressure and incentives for results as an excuse for unethical actions. Speak up when you see such unintended consequences and work together to devise better incentive systems and associated checks and balances.

When we anticipate unintended consequences, we can often prevent them.

Sending the right message.

When cyanide was found in a few Tylenol capsules in one city several years ago, Johnson and Johnson quickly stopped production throughout the country and suspended sales until it could develop a tamper proof cap. Across the country, J&J personnel shared a consistent message rooted in its "Credo," a shared commitment that puts customers first. Although the company took a short-term loss, the decision earned customer confidence and loyalty in the longer term. It's now a classic case of values in action.

Act Decisively on Problems.

Take action when things go wrong.

When we ask for feedback, we need to do something with what we learn!

If you find a problem, report it. If you're in charge, correct it. If disciplinary action is needed, do it promptly and consistently. That way, everyone gets the message that you take ethics seriously.

Nothing undermines confidence in ethical standards more quickly than the impression that wrongdoing is tolerated. Management may impose strong discipline, even firing people, but you won't necessarily learn the details. As employees, remember that management can not always reveal exactly what happened. As managers, try to share as much information as possible without violating the privacy rights of those affected.

Creative leaders find ways to get the message across. One CEO sent a letter to all employees generally describing some unethical behaviors and explaining that people had been severely disciplined for such actions. Those close to the situation probably knew who was affected, but the general communication ensured that everyone understood that firm action was taken.

In another company, several people were terminated and many employees were shocked because those who lost their jobs were well liked. Plant leadership conducted training programs for all employees, using case discussions based on the actions that led to the discipline. Without naming names or opening specific files, the managers were able to explain to employees that everyone who was disciplined had done things that the employees said were clearly wrong in the hypothetical case discussions.

When we address ethical lapses decisively and consistently, we build confidence and trust in our shared commitments.

Competitive realities sometimes require painful decisions. Ethics is not just for the "good times."

Promise honest answers, then deliver on your promises.

This suggestion is specifically for supervisors and other leaders. Feedback from informal conversations, employee surveys or a confidential telephone system should be treated seriously.

Find answers to the questions. If it's confidential, say so. If it's a problem you haven't solved yet, admit it. If the concern is unfounded, explain why. There is no substitute for honest answers.

When you don't know the answer to a question –or the question itself just makes you uncomfortable– it is tempting to "waffle." You may brush the question off with a vague reply or you might just postpone an answer indefinitely. That undermines trust. Honesty is far better, even if it means saying "I don't know" or "That's not something I think I can deal with right now."

People understand why some things might be confidential or unresolved. But they expect leaders to be forthright, to treat them with respect as partners in a shared enterprise. And, they can spot "spin" a mile away.

Honest answers build understanding, trust and commitment to shared goals.

Learn From Mistakes

Face reality and acknowledge gaps.

Mistakes are part of the learning process. Honestly talking about where we fall short creates opportunity to improve.

If a process or piece of equipment isn't working properly, ignoring it makes matters worse. That's also true about individual and group performance that falls short of stated, measurable goals.

An employee spots a foreign substance in a batch of material, but the supervisor insists on meeting shipping targets. Later the product is recalled at great expense and regulatory penalties.

A bookkeeper questions how reserves are allocated but is over ruled to meet pressures for quarterly profit. The pattern continues until front-page news announces the company's restated earnings, financial penalties and a management shake up.

Just watch the business news for a few weeks and the evidence is regularly there –sweeping problems under the rug only makes a bigger mess to clean up later.

You'll be more responsible –ethically responsible, financially responsible, operationally responsible—if you acknowledge problems when they occur and focus on fixing them.

That means sharing information and owning up to mistakes right away. For supervisors and other leaders, it also means fostering an environment of open communication and focus on solutions.

Facing up to problems honestly is the first step toward solving them and making improvements.

The traditionalist prefers foolishness frozen into custom to foolishness fresh off the vine.

– D. Sutton

Take risks.

To do our best, we sometimes try new ideas without knowing if they'll work. Testing a new idea with a co-worker, seeking advice about a tough challenge, taking reasonable risks to learn something valuable regardless of the outcome –steps like these are essential to achieving our best performance.

You're more willing to take such risks when you know you can count on each other.

You naturally worry, "Will I be penalized if I fail?" And, your supervisor wonders, "What if my employee's risk taking affects my performance goals?"

Neither of you can resolve these questions precisely because every situation is different. If the answers were entirely clear ahead of time, there would be no risk.

That's why mutual trust is necessary. In a sense, both you and your supervisor are saying, "I'll take a leap of faith if you will."

There is no road map for risk-taking. But fostering an environment of honest communication and mutual trust enables everyone to keep testing the limit.

As a supervisor or manager, you must also avoid "shooting the messenger" or unfairly punishing someone for a mistake. The goal is to learn from the experience and not repeat it.

If we never take risks, we will under achieve. Genuine trust creates the "safety net" that inspires the risk taking needed to improve processes and products in dramatic ways.

Everyday Ethics
Summing Up

Do the right thing and never compromise your integrity — at work, at home, and in the community.

Treat others as you would like to be treated.

When all of us act responsibly like this everyday, we build an atmosphere of mutual respect and trust. That, in turn, lays the foundation for achieving together far more than any one of us could do alone. Because we rely on each other, we focus on accomplishing shared goals instead of worrying about another person's "agenda." We do our own tasks mindful of the bigger picture.

Together we sustain this trust by understanding and living the practical day to day meaning of our shared values and commitments. And, if we're serious in our commitment and honest with ourselves, we know we sometimes fall short. Maintaining trust means solving problems and finding ways to improve on a continuous basis.

Every one of the behaviors outlined in this book can help you to do your part. And when each of us acts responsibly, it works for all of us.

Responsible management has always been the right thing to do. In the long run, it is also a business necessity.

Notes

To Learn More

Built to Last: Successful Habits of Visionary Companies, James C. Collins and Jerry I. Porras (New York: HarperCollins, 1994).

Ethics and Excellence: Cooperation and Integrity in Business, Robert C. Solomon (New York: Oxford University Press, 1993).

Ethics Matters: How to Implement Values-Driven Management, Dawn-Marie Driscoll and W. Michael Hoffman (Waltham, MA: Bentley College, 2000).

The Ethical Edge: Tales of Organizations That Have Faced Moral Crises, Dawn-Marie Driscoll, W. Michael Hoffman and Edward S. Petry (New York: Master Media, 1995).

The Responsible Manager: Practical Strategies for Ethical Decision-Making. Michael Rion. Available from Resources for Ethics and Management.

The Soul of a Business: Managing for Profit and the Common Good, Tom Chappell (New York: Bantam Books, 1993).

Notes

1 "Communication" brochure cited with permission from Olin Corporation.
2 James Collins and Jerry Porras, Built to Last: Successful Habits of Visionary Companies (HarperBusiness, 1994).
3 "Principles for Business," Caux Roundtable Secretariat, 1156 Fifteenth Street NW, Suite 910, Washington, DC 20005-1704.
4 Attributed to Warren Bennis, cited in Rosabeth Moss Kanter and Barry A. Stein, Life in Organizations: Workplaces as People Experience Them (New York: Basic Books, 1979) p. 315.

Everyday Ethics

1-99 copies	$9.95 per book
100-999 copies	$8.95 per book
1000-2499 copies	$7.95 per book
2500-4999 copies	$6.95 per book
5000-9999 copies	$5.95 per book
over 10000 copies	$4.95 per book

Order Form

Resources for Ethics and Management
14 Cornell Road
West Hartford, CT 06107-2905
Tel (860) 521-9233 Fax (860) 521-4697
E-mail mrion@attglobal.net
www.rionethics.com

Everyday Ethics: Putting Values into Action

_____copies @ $_____each

SHIP TO:

Name_____

Title_____

Organization_____

P.O. Box_____Zip_____

Street Address_____Zip_____

City/ State_____

Country_____

Phone (___)_____P.O.#_____

Applicable sales tax, shipping and handling charges will be added.

Orders may be placed by mail, fax or e-mail.